BENJAMIN BANNEKER

Pioneering Scientist

BY GINGER WADSWORTH

ILLUSTRATIONS BY CRAIG ORBACK

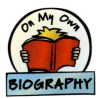

On My Own

BIOGRAPHY

Carolrhoda Books, Inc./Minneapolis

The illustrator would like to thank the models who were used for the oil paintings, especially J,Khaylaughn Lewis, Thaddeus Turner, and Fredrick Brown, who represent the various ages of Benjamin, as well as Gary and Eileen Orback and the Lewis family, who represent assorted characters. Thanks also to Jessica Silks for her help with photography.

The photographs on page 46 appear courtesy of © U.S. Postal Service (top) and © Bettmann/CORBIS (bottom).

Text copyright © 2003 by Ginger Wadsworth
Illustrations copyright © 2003 by Craig Orback

This book is available in two editions:
Library binding by Carolrhoda Books, Inc., a division of Lerner Publishing Group
Soft cover by First Avenue Editions, an imprint of Lerner Publishing Group
241 First Avenue North
Minneapolis, MN 55401 U.S.A.

Website address: www.lernerbooks.com

Library of Congress Cataloging-in-Publication Data

Wadsworth, Ginger.
    Benjamin Banneker / by Ginger Wadsworth ; illustrations by Craig Orback.
      p.   cm. — (On my own biography)
    Summary: Introduces Benjamin Banneker, a free black man of the eighteenth century who loved to learn and used his knowledge and observations to build a wooden clock, write an almanac, and help survey the streets of Washington, D.C.
    ISBN: 0–87614–916–6 (lib. bdg. : alk. paper)
    ISBN: 0–87614–104–1 (pbk. : alk. paper)
    1. Banneker, Benjamin, 1731–1806—Juvenile literature. 2. Astronomers—United States—Biography—Juvenile literature. 3. African American scientists—Biography—Juvenile literature. [1. Banneker, Benjamin, 1731–1806. 2. Astronomers. 3. African Americans—Biography.] I. Orback, Craig, ill. II. Title. III. Series.
QB36.B22 W34 2003
520'.92—dc21   2002000985

Manufactured in the United States of America
1 2 3 4 5 6 – SP – 08 07 06 05 04 03

In memory of William "Unk" Brobeck,
Pioneer Inventor and Engineer —G.W.

For Michael O'Dwyer in New Zealand,
another inquisitive mind —C.S.O.

Maryland

1737

Benjamin Banneker was working
on his family's tobacco farm.
It was hard work for a six-year-old boy.
The sun baked his back
as he cut weeds with his hoe.
He picked bugs off the big, flat leaves.
Sometimes he counted the bugs,
just before he squished them.

He counted all the rows of tobacco
plants on the farm.
He even counted logs in the cabin he shared
with his parents and three sisters.
Counting made the lonely work
a little more fun.

At supper, Benjamin listened to stories
about his family.

Benjamin's grandmother was white.
She had been a servant long ago.
She worked for many years without pay.
Benjamin's grandfather was black.
In Africa, he had been the son of a king.
In America, he had been a slave.
Benjamin's father had been a slave, too.
But no one in Benjamin's family
was a slave anymore.
Their owners had set them free.
Now the Bannekers owned this farm.
Benjamin and his family were lucky.
Most black men, women, and children
in America were slaves.
They did not own anything.

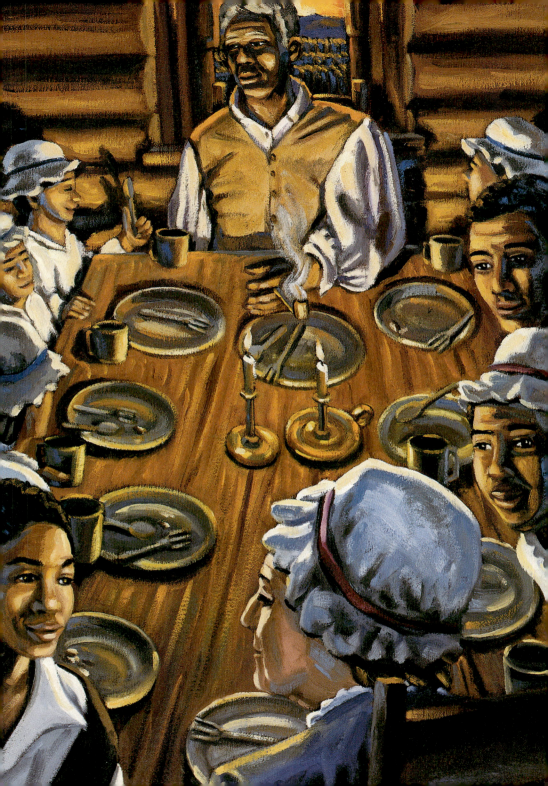

After supper, Benjamin sat

with Grandmother Molly in her cabin.

A fire heated the little house.

Candles lit the room.

Grandmother Molly opened her Bible.

It was the only book she owned.

Grandmother was teaching Benjamin to read.

Benjamin was a fast learner.

Everyone in the family was proud of him.

He could read and write.

And he was especially good

at doing math problems.

After Grandmother Molly had taught

Benjamin everything she could,

she sent him to school.

Benjamin had never seen so many books!
Most of the students at school had white skin,
like Grandmother Molly.
Everyone sat on benches
and listened to the teacher.
Sometimes they did math problems.
Other times, they read from books.
The teacher even let Benjamin take
some books home.
Benjamin worked hard and learned a lot.
After school, he did chores.
Then, if he was not too sleepy,
he could read his school books.

At night, Benjamin lay on his bed
and looked out the window.
Stars sparkled in the inky-black sky.
Some were brighter than others,
and Benjamin wondered why.
Some groups of stars looked like
animals or shapes.
Sometimes a star seemed to shoot
across the sky.
Benjamin wondered why.

The Clock Maker

After only four years of school,
Benjamin had to quit.
He was young and strong.
His family needed him
to work on the farm full time.

14

But school had made Benjamin
hungry to learn.
He still kept his eyes on the sky.
Sometimes he did hard
math problems in the dirt.
He used a stick instead of a pencil.
At night, Benjamin read books by candlelight.

Like most farmers,

Benjamin told time by watching

the position of the sun.

But sometimes the sun was hidden

behind trees or clouds.

Clocks had been around for a long time.

But in the 1750s,

only rich people had clocks.

Benjamin decided to make his own.

When he was 20 years old,

Benjamin borrowed a friend's pocket watch.

He took it apart and studied each tiny piece.

How did the thin hands go around

and around, ticking off each minute?

He drew a sketch of each piece.

Then he carved new parts out of wood.

He worked on his clock

through the winter and summer.

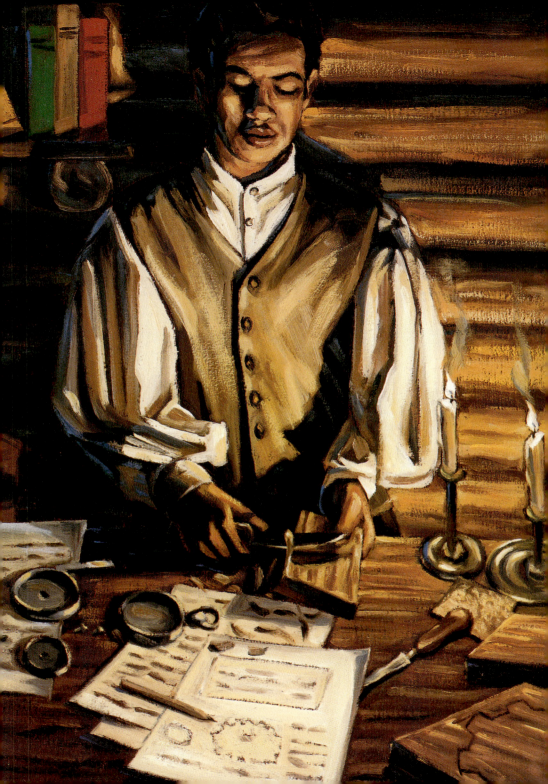

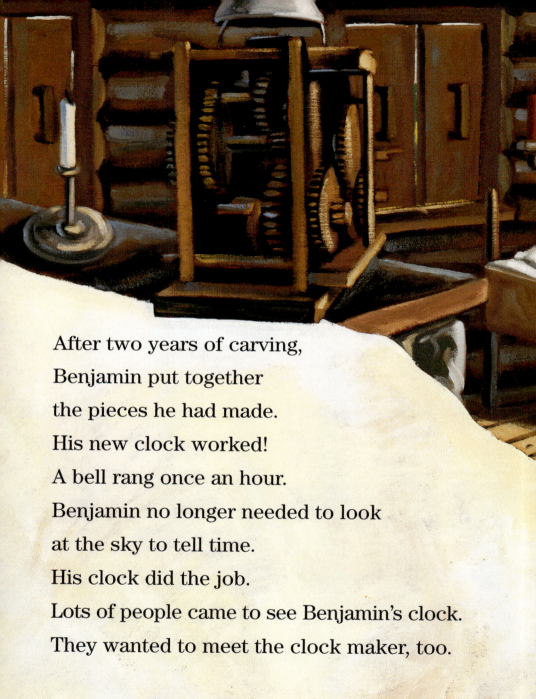

After two years of carving,
Benjamin put together
the pieces he had made.
His new clock worked!
A bell rang once an hour.
Benjamin no longer needed to look
at the sky to tell time.
His clock did the job.
Lots of people came to see Benjamin's clock.
They wanted to meet the clock maker, too.

When Benjamin was 27 years old,

the lonely farm life got even lonelier.

His father died.

His sisters had married and moved away.

And Grandmother Molly had died.

Only Benjamin and his mother were left

to do all the farm work.

There was so much to do,

Benjamin had little time for studying.

Sometimes he stayed up late

and read his math books.

Some nights he played his flute or violin

and thought about his father.

Benjamin began to make friends with
other farmers who lived nearby.
Many could not read or write.
They didn't know much about math, either.
Benjamin showed his new friends
how to weigh their tobacco crop.
He helped them figure out
how much it was worth.
He also helped them write letters.
Benjamin often met other farmers
at a nearby store.
They read newspapers there and talked
about the tough questions of farming.
Was it time to plow?
Was it going to snow again?
Was it too early to plant seeds?
Maybe someday Benjamin could help
his friends with these questions, too.

Revolution!

1775

After Benjamin's mother died,

he had to run the whole farm by himself.

It was harder than ever to find time to study.

At least he had friends at the store

to keep him company.

Important news gave Benjamin
and his friends a lot to talk about.
Maryland was one of 13 American
colonies ruled by Great Britain.
Many Americans thought the colonies
should be free to rule themselves.
They did not like paying taxes
to the British king.

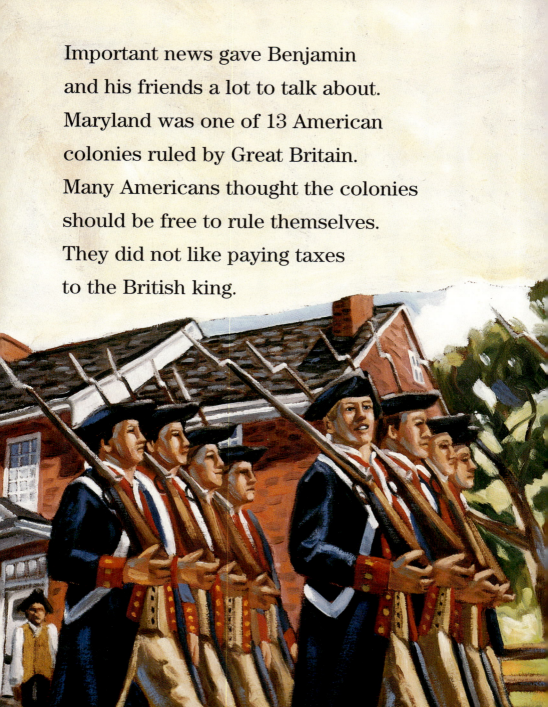

In April, British soldiers attacked
Americans in Massachusetts.
The Americans quickly formed an army.
George Washington was their leader.
Soldiers marched up and down the roads
near Benjamin's farm.
A war had begun.

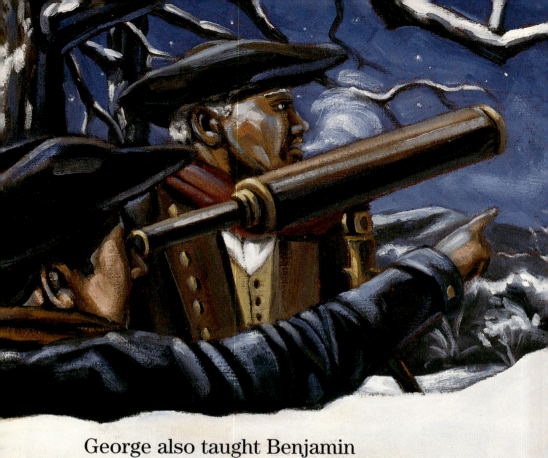

George also taught Benjamin
about astronomy.
Astronomy is the science of studying
the Sun, Moon, stars, and planets.
George even had a telescope.
Benjamin had always wondered
about the stars.

Now he learned that the brightest stars
were not stars at all.
They were distant planets.
Benjamin studied George's astronomy books.
He learned how to follow the positions
of the planets.
With this information, Benjamin could tell
what the weather would be like next year.
His new knowledge also made him
a better surveyor.

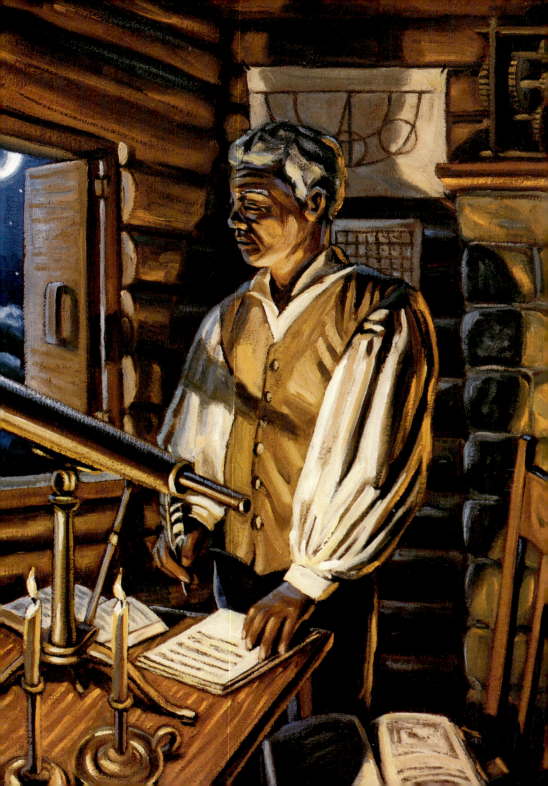

There was so much to learn!
Sometimes Benjamin stayed up
studying all night.
He thought about his farmer friends.
Benjamin thought he could help them
with their farming questions.
He wanted to write an almanac.
In the 1700s, almanacs were
important books.
New ones came out every year.
They gave people information
for every day in the year.
Almanacs had calendars
and dates for planting and harvesting.
They also told what the weather
would be like the next year.
Some almanacs had poems, stories,
recipes, and news.

Benjamin dipped his pen in the ink bottle
over and over again.

Piles of paper covered his table.

On some, he had written math problems.

Some had notes about the sky
and the weather.

When the rooster crowed,
Benjamin put away his work.

It was time to milk the cows.

In 1790, President Washington chose a site
to build America's capital city.
The area was called the District of Columbia.
It was only a few hours away
from Benjamin's farm.
The president needed surveyors
to plan the streets.
The top surveyor on the job was
Andrew Ellicott, George's cousin.
Andrew knew that Benjamin was very good
at surveying and astronomy.
He asked Benjamin to help him.

Helping to survey the capital was
a great honor for Benjamin.
Very few black people in the 1790s got
a chance to do such important work.
And it was fun, too.
Benjamin loved using Andrew's excellent
surveying tools.
Benjamin worked during the cold, damp,
winter nights.
Sometimes he slept only
a few hours in his tent.
After three months, the work and weather
were wearing Benjamin down.
He was almost 60 years old.
He loved his job,
but he was ready to go home.
It was time to finish his almanac.

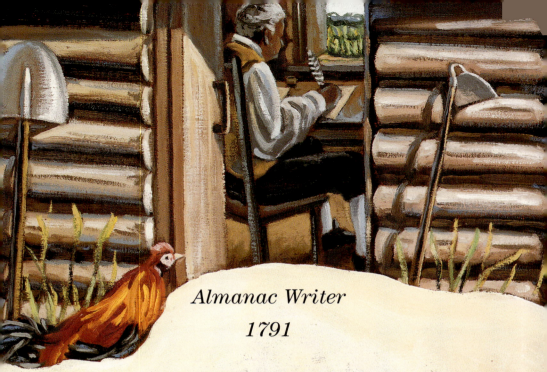

Almanac Writer

1791

At home, Benjamin wrote and wrote.

When he stopped, it was only to sharpen

his pen tip with his knife.

He checked his math many times.

Sometimes he forgot to do the farm chores.

It took Benjamin four months

to write an almanac for the year 1792.

His book was packed with information

that people needed—especially farmers.

Benjamin made four copies of his almanac
in his best penmanship.

He sent one copy to Thomas Jefferson.

Jefferson was the secretary of state
of the United States.

He was also a farmer, like Benjamin.

Like many white farmers,
Jefferson owned slaves.

Benjamin sent a long letter to Jefferson
along with the almanac.
He wrote that slavery was cruel.
Black people deserved to be treated
the same as white people.
He argued that no one should own slaves—
not even important American leaders.
A few weeks later, Benjamin received
a letter from Jefferson.
Jefferson thanked Benjamin
for his almanac.
He said he hoped things
would improve in the future
for black people.
But Jefferson did not free his slaves.

A book publisher wanted to print
and sell Benjamin's almanac.
It was the first published almanac
written by a black person.
Printed on the cover were the words
Benjamin Banneker's Almanac.
The publisher sold many copies,
and Benjamin became famous.
People wrote him letters,
thanking him for the helpful information.
They came to his cabin to meet him,
just as they had when he built the clock.
Benjamin stayed busy.
He had to write an almanac for 1793.
And he wrote one for the next year, too.
He wrote a new almanac every year
for six years.

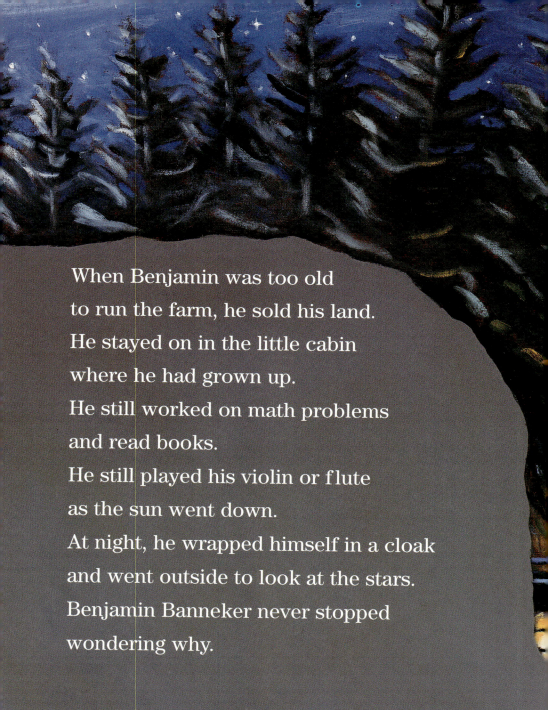

When Benjamin was too old
to run the farm, he sold his land.
He stayed on in the little cabin
where he had grown up.
He still worked on math problems
and read books.
He still played his violin or flute
as the sun went down.
At night, he wrapped himself in a cloak
and went outside to look at the stars.
Benjamin Banneker never stopped
wondering why.

In 1980, the United States Post Office issued a Benjamin Banneker stamp.

Benjamin Bannaker's PENNSYLVANIA, DELAWARE, MARY-LAND, AND VIRGINIA ALMANAC, FOR THE YEAR of our LORD 1795; Being the Third after Leap-Year.

BANNAKER.

PHILADELPHIA:
Printed for WILLIAM GIBBONS, Cherry Street

The title page from one of Benjamin's almanacs. He spelled his name *Bannaker*, but it was later changed to *Banneker*.